MW00424408

Black Leapt In

Winner of the Barrow Street Press Poetry Prize,
selected by Phillis Levin

Black Leapt In

Chris Forhan

Barrow Street Press
New York City

©2009 by Chris Forhan
All rights reserved

Designed by Robert Drummond
Cover painting "Wave Connecting Dark Pits" (1993)
        by Tom Aprile
Chris Forhan photo by Alessandra Lynch

Published by Barrow Street Press
Distributed by:
        Barrow Street
        P.O. Box 1831
        Murray Hill Station
        New York, NY 10156

First Edition

Library of Congress control number: 2009926605

ISBN 978-0-9819876-0-6

For my mother, Ange Forhan Scott,
and in memory of my father,
Edward Michael Forhan,
1929-1973

CONTENTS

This Time

Say it hasn't happened yet. One thin cloud is pinned to the blue.
Birds drowse in the oak out back. The priest's shoe gleams black, no
      mud on it.

Say it. Nothing worth weeping for has slipped in.
A moth's wing ticks at a window, that's it.

To say so, to gaze with longing at my own unclosing eye,
to go back, unsmudge the start. That's it.

No place at the table unset this time, no heart in the house
unaccounted for. And what then. What now.

The Case Against Me

Boyhood was a blue sky with a blimp in it,
a bucket of chocolate, bottomless pool of noon

I paddled on. OK, that's mostly made up,
if I think about it. If I think, a girl unblurs,

the one down the block who kept snakes
in wire cages. If I think, my father

sleeps in his car, ice gathering on the windows,
in the hinges, sealing him in. How sweet to believe

the wind keened for him then, and the sunset
donned a tactful sash of swallows. Who knows.

I turned, wouldn't talk—couldn't, what with
the fat frog that lodged on my tongue,

sudden lump against the roof of my mouth,
my teeth. It took years of distraction

to jimmy him, ease him out with a pinkie.
What a project! His eyes, when at last

I saw them, were happily expressionless.
The heart gets sad, you slap it.

That billowy thing in flames back there?
That's not my circus tent. Never seen it.

Toward a Full Accounting

The year of stepping out from the matinee
onto the bright sidewalk and waiting
for our mothers to pull up in tan station wagons.
In the chill air, sharp against our cheeks,
the chance that they would not come.
They came. The year of the flattened grass
that made a path to the ball field, of birds
who were blind to the house we built them
and nailed to a branch, twelve dark doors.
I was a real boy, made of sturdy pressboard.
I can't speak for the others. Only say
the word, and I shall be healed, I prayed,
my illness unrevealed to me. I pulled the string
too tight and snapped my kite's cross stick.
I wore a mop-head wig for the talent show,
this being the year I was an expert on mop-head wigs
and sea anemones and their feeding habits.
My deportment and attention: satisfactory.
Frayed book bag, stolen bike, my best friend's
basement, its scent of eucalyptus and dust,
ashtrays in the shape of tropical fish. Mahogany box
of poker chips. Pope Paul VI in his frame.
I liked to look at him—delicate hand against
his chest, the face—but he was looking elsewhere.

Prayer Before Sleep

Straight A's on arithmetic quizzes, your cheek gets ground
into the concrete down here, Sir. Thank You

for sending only Your smallest monsters to find me
and Your giant silence, thank You for that, within it

I accept that the Beatles won't sing in my rec room ever
and my gerbil will not unstiffen and nibble through his shoebox.

My teeth—I'd forgotten them—the braces are working,
don't worry, and my hands, my back, no problem. I will bear

Your son across Thornton Creek when You send Him
should You lower Him into my neighborhood. Let

the capsule of astronauts splash down gently,
let me stay friends forever with William and Phil

and with Jenny, a discovery of late, by Your grace.
If Dad and Mom laughing today is Your doing,

thanks. My sister's no bother, really. You haven't yet
taken my soul in my sleep, You let me lie in my bed like this,

the window lifted. Whatever that sweetness in the breeze is,
as if it's still summer, thank You for that, and for the Beatles.

School Carnival

I was curled inside the owl's mouth and cold
when I woke one morning. The next
I was writhing atop a wire cage with a wolf in it.
Then hunched in a coal car lurching backward,
bathed in hot rain. It was spring. My mother
wouldn't shake me from sleep anymore—I was older
and set my own alarm.
                            When I entered, the classroom
was dark, beaded curtain clicking behind me.
The air smelled of incense and pencils.
Our desks were gone. Had they ever been there?
A paper lantern glowed maroon where the globe had been.
Something will happen, the fortune teller said—
the principal's secretary in a black wig and rouge.
It will be something ordinary. You won't forget it.

Having Crept from My Bed

Pressed against coats in the family room
closet, I peered through the door slats
at my father watching television.

An astronaut waved from a white convertible,
confetti in his crewcut. He'd been
where the planets crash and whirl.

I might have been a moth or shoe,
not breathing, not flinching, as the day
rolled away on its slow wheel. My father

aimed the remote. A man was lowered
to the ocean floor, clamped in a bathysphere.
Down there the fish don't have eyes.

My father lifted his drink. We watched
morning sun burn mist from the encampment.
The colonel sent word to take the hill.

It is possible to be born a prince
and slip into each day as into a golden robe.
It is possible to feel your chest fill with ash.

Something was ending. The black screen,
scroll of the credits, blue smoke swirling
from the tip of my father's cigarette. A tornado

skittered like a phonograph needle over farmland.
My father set down his glass. Then a woman in an apron
was standing where her home had been.

My Father's Curriculum Vitae

*I was handed the pamphlet of maxims, took it into my heart,
        folks did that then.*

Was grandson, pal, penitent, fulfilled the contract.

*Distinguished myself in trig and cigarettes, in whistling whatever
        had topped the Hit Parade.*

*Plucked my brother from the lake, tucked him into the lining of my
        cap on the chance he'd undrown one day.*

*Put on the soldier's gear, shipped island-ward, you should have seen
        me in my dress whites, dozed at my post just the one time.*

*Picked a gray suit and a brown one, stood rigid while the pins
        slipped in.*

Clicked the briefcase shut open shut.

Wielded the slide rule, wielded the silver shoehorn.

Come to me, Christ, I cried, there's mud in my eye sockets.

*Woke to rustling—my dead mother, my gone father, back as two
        birds in a fluster above my head.*

*Roused the children from bed, showed them how each planet spins,
        distant, arranged blue marbles on the carpet.*

Dug pennies from my pocket, tossed them into a bowl.

*Entered the bedroom once, ready to speak to her, sat on the floor,
    rocked and said nothing.*

*Lowered the Ford's idle, tightened the Chevy's brakes, watched the
    bubble fidget in the spirit level.*

Whispered farewell, farewell into my own ear.

Slept late on Sundays, then Mondays, then couldn't sleep.

*Knelt in a field of strawberries, damp dirt, damp leaves, pretty wife
    in the row to my right, my good children—*

*Lifted a bit of that redness to my lips, little thought in it, just taking
    sweetness in, sweet shock of not knowing, of not remembering.
    Pretty wife.*

Vanishing Act

Each bed with a child in it, or his wife,
his brain lined with sleeping bees,

my father is having to leave the house
with delicacy, easing the dead bolt open

in the dark. The house exhales him.
I'm thinking of a driving lay-up, of a girl

in homeroom, blue necklace, brown skin.
Transistor radio on my pillow, volume low.

I know some things, not enough. My eyes
are closed, I'm listening hard, that song

again, *Knock down the old gray wall,*
my father standing beside his car—gone,

key in his hand, snowflakes in his hair.
At dawn, an Indian-head test pattern will stare

from the TV, the freezer will churn out
its automatic ice. On the windowsill

an iris in a vase will have taken
the last water into its cut stem. I will

notice it, how it is there, and had
stood there the whole time, that flower.

Postmortem

The clean things I cleaned them again could not keep them clean
calculated quarterly earnings weighed them against the five-year
strategic plan
gripped the paddle with both hands worked the riffles
fell into a spill of sleep
won't wake

no wind where I am
it isn't wind whirling blank leaves settling them in my hair
and upon my eyes
I'm beyond cause
say I signed my name to nothing

something I remember is thirst
frost at dawn the front steps slick with it
my mother was nowhere
who knew her
in the air the taste of iron and necessity
error prowled after me leaping from roof to roof
I was thirsty

a carp afloat in a clear bag gleamed gold
I was a boy then holding the bag in my lap in the backseat
someone my silent grandfather maybe at the wheel
gold goes
I knew that
I'd seen ash sift through winter air and fill the ditch
night rose inside that car the fish glistening

say I'm asleep
a carp in stale water
I was awake once a son a husband
I was thirsty I worked I was good
waited said little
and the ladle came late no milk in it

Black

Sludge at the edge of the field, still water, slat fence
and its rickrack shadow. Trowel tongue.
Tulip rooted in black, cricket soaked in it.
Mask of the cedar waxwing. Snipe's eye, fly's face.
A nudge does it, if you're young enough.
My jaw dropped and black leapt in,
black spleen, black brain, black car
pulling out of the driveway, turning at the top of the hill,
then noon, black in its blue suit.

Dream: Natural Law

The sea is clean, unscuffed: it looks convincing, the sun like hearsay
      slipping into it.
Donde estan sus padres? a small girl asks me, pink plastic shovel in her
      fist, the paint of her dress still wet in places.
I have no answer, I'm glitter, I'm hardly here.
She's glad and kneels as if to dig, the sky blushing crimson, like a hint.

None of this matters, so soon it will shatter me. A sprinkle of
      graveyard dirt will appear in my sock drawer.
Mr. Glib will consider the law and become shy of speech, persuasive,
      as some rocks are.

If a horse drinks old water, winter will be hard.
If milk won't whip, it's got a witch in it.
If a child says his prayers in reverse, he'll wake with no father.

I woke with no father. I knew what the sea wouldn't say. What I'd lost,
      it had taken.

The Fall

Then a stone appeared in my cereal bowl and the hoodoo hit:
green drained from the lawn, the font water iced over.
The hothouse in lockdown, bus fumes blacked the snow.

Therefore: my run for class president, the hundred handmade
campaign signs, blue Hush Puppies, unfortunate corduroys.
Therefore: my week as a pile of smoldering leaves.

My mousehood, my tail-time, the gnawed linoleum.
45's wobbled around the spindle—I did the Idiot, I did the Worm.
I blathered on Saturday, on Sunday kept quiet. Dad

would not be back, so I slid his desk drawer open; it was filled
with blank paper. I took up his ruler, then set it down. I took up
his pen—it turned to fire in my hands. I took up his pen.

Thirty-Year Elegy

He paddled out, let the swell swallow him. Blind grappling hook
in my brain dragging the silt for him: it's what he left me.

One thing bothered him into being, packed muscle and blood in him.
It ripens the grape into wine, makes the park swarm with orphans.

A mind that won't forget, that was my father's gift: fingering
each misery like a fat coin, then dropping it into his pocket.

His being back now—bashful, but ready to tell it all, uncorking
a bottle of something rare to share with his children—I did that.

Self-Portrait

1

A spoonful of ooze, an idea an atom had,
I found myself

tugging soaked galoshes off, rising
to attention in creased slacks and neckerchief,
a cowlicked loyalist to the pack.

2

The priest sang in Latin. He didn't ask my opinion.

The slim missal my mother pressed to my palm
she longed to offer to a better boy,
the twin I'd killed in the womb.

3

The future was a fixed thing coming.

A gust of swallows
swooped and ascended, looping
around the steeple, over the rectory,
into the leafy secrecy of a spring willow.

4

We are indiscretions, a bother to God.
Try choking back that thick smoke.

5

Try shaking my father and sister down from a tree
or scouring the arroyo and ridge for them.
They're not at large anymore.

He wearied of mirrors, traded his face for forgetfulness.
She's safe now, her skull full of flowers.

6

And shall I singe my tongue on them?
Be a glutton for nothingness?

Or shall I make myself at home,
leap and feast, do squirrel-work—

shall I pledge allegiance to sleep, unlikely
eternity blossoming with balloons?

7

I'm in the teeth of something befuddled and mute and furious.

I'm wishing for a clarity of mind
with fire in it: attentiveness
that lives amid loss and loves it.

I'm watching dawn arrive again to whiten the salt flats,
a slash of red, some wing—gone before it sings.

Climbing Down

My foot is on the ladder to the cellar where the bear lives,
where the smell of old headlines and hair tonic
gathers in corners, and Christmas lights bulge from a box.

What year was it? Untangling the lights, guiding the wire
as it rose, orange and blue bulbs vanishing past
the roof's edge. My father somewhere up there on his knees.

In the back of a comic book, a ghost I could send away for
to amaze my friends. Controlled by strings.
They won't be able to tell it from the real thing.

I pasted paper in the shape of my house onto cardboard
and drew in a garden near the drainage ditch. I painted the Mass
at St. Mary's church and gave the priest my father's face.

I was following a rope into sleep, then out
toward morning. I didn't mean to awaken
this way, climbing down through the dark, something

shifting about below, my heart heavy with ice.
The idea was to keep what I loved from harm.
The idea was to keep what I loved.

Hopeful Green Stuff

We'd been issued our folk guitars and fake books, striped pants and
    puka shell bracelets.

Summer's vast expanse unfurling, bare feet stained green by the
    fresh-cut grass, fingers contorting toward the major chords.

Wasps thronged the melon balls, brambles strangled the garden.
    We turned golden.

O lush boredom, blue extravagant sky, transistor insisting *Someday
    we'll walk in the rays of a beautiful sun* . . .

Moms were there, pouring chilled milk. When dark descended, dads
    raised flames in the pit.

We circled it, we sang along, there was nothing we were learning.
    We were earning our ribbons for participation.

Testament

Being made to drink vinegar from a sponge,
that part was true. And feeling bad for the lepers.
Being a Cub Scout with a glue gun
in a paneled den, one jar of silver glitter,
one of blue. My wings then—with duct tape
I strapped them down, near the backstop
I rolled in the dust to muss them.
The cave's mouth glowed gold but
I missed it, I was tucked in, my brain
was filled to bursting with the TV listings.
I rode a red bike with a warning bell,
I stood in the lunch line while a hole
was punched in my milk ticket. Ducks
vanished into the mist upon the wading pool—
some sorcery, some hopefulness. I lowered
my head to accept the canvas bag
of newspapers, I crossed the creaky footbridge
to Bill O'Meara's house, a pale pink light
on everything. No scribe for all that then.
A hurt squirrel pulled its bulk across the grass,
I placed my hand upon it, I washed right after.
That was not I among the reeds. I was
with the others on the patio playing Parcheesi,
I was slouched in the back of the school bus,
thumbing the transistor's volume knob.
I wore the satiny green trunks of our team.

Fourth Grade Science

Improbable: our toes and shoes, the tongues and laces.
No answer for that. Or for the bird at the window.
A finch? It ignores us, it knows its business.

The ball field's puddled, muddy. Some floodwater
might have brought us here—me to my seat
near the dangling rope of the window shade,

Willy to his seat near the door, Maddie
to the shirt she's worn all week: pink, a bunny on it.
My *Marvels of Nature* book proclaims

the inked-in names of those who owned it once.
Ghosts. The name of my new best friend: Paul Ringo.
Two Beatles! What rule was revoked for that to happen,

or anything: a fish with a saw for a head,
monkey-bar rust that rubs off on our palms,
the scar on the crossing guard's throat, licked there by fire,

Miss Lagerquist passing the chalk across the blackboard
in perfect cursive, bracelets jangling. Why isn't she
married? The book says juice oozes from its body—

with this, the snail makes a house. O Willy, Maddie, Paul,
we just got here: already a blind bear, at a hundred yards,
would recognize us for what we are.

Where I Come From

No sadness. Secrecy's a sweet wine we sip from one cup.
Someone sits alone in her car in the dark, listening to the engine tick.
Now she enters the house.

A small thing hauls its bruised body beneath a hedge.
Some branches tremble, then don't.
Dinner's in the fridge, chocolate money's in the Easter grass.

If you pick up a crooked pin, it means good fortune.
If a child doesn't cry when christened, he's doubly blessed.
If you're asked, Dad's traveling, no phones on the tundra.

O wolves circling the curbside trash, you don't bother us.
You're boys who've come back. We knew you in your cute suits,
carrying your basketball shoes to school in paper bags.

O girls whirling in place on the lawn like mad flowers,
you're just our daughters, you have no worries,
you can't be widows at this age.

Family Vacation

Down the coast road we went, wheel steady—
Dad steady, whistling Roger Miller tunes—
suitcases strapped to the roof, our car the color
of a package forgotten on the seat of a train.

We kids in the cramped back squabbled,
were deputized to spot a farm animal, water tower,
bus. I found the tower and saw myself
sitting atop it as we passed. Mom adjusted

her sun shade. We were a glint of metal on a rock
spinning through the infinite. Near Eureka
we stopped, leaned on the bumper,
peeled grapefruit with a pocketknife.
All around, strange license plates, gold on black.

In a motel room, the kids on cots, Dad
shook us awake with his sleeping, his
strangled gasps and wheezes, he was off
on private business. Moonlit water glasses
stood by the sink in paper hoods.

Lobsters in a tank, San Francisco,
the bound claws swung slowly.

In the lake cabin's eaves, a family
of carpenter bees stirred while I slipped
in the shower—my chin clipped
the soap holder, knocked loose
two baby teeth. I was working
to capacity, days away from losing
my plastic souvenir cutlass, no pirate I.

O 1965, Herman's Hermits on the radio,
Dad veering the station wagon onto
the wrong road, traffic swarming. I can't
see a solution, he said. He won't unbudge,

he's stuck in that summer, mumbling over a map
or leaning back in a pool chair, face
in the shade, cigarette dangling
Andy Capp fashion forever from his lower lip.

A word with you, sir. I want
my toy back. I want my teeth.

The Woods

Beyond the tracing paper and safety scissors and balled-up socks in
       the closet,
beyond the bleached sheets of the sickbed, dry toast, purple syrup down
       the throat,

past walls and lawns, where the street stopped and dirt began, and
       daytime dark,
where branches interlocked like fingers high above me, where older boys

brought their noises, war whoops and cherry bombs, leaving behind
shattered bottles and a matchbook, a single match still in it ...

Of five brothers, one held his breath all night and day. Another
swallowed the sea. Another was drawn toward the woods and found

the match—I lit it; it leapt from my hand, seethed into gold
and smoke, rolled through bushes, blackened the grass. Fear

flared. You have burned my acre, said the Lord, but you did not
think to do so. Look, look. You have made it beautiful.

Bureau Inspection

A boy is the product of a big idea
concealed from him. He is taught
to fold his shirts so the arms bend back,
then store them in bureau drawers.
A mother loves her son but looks
askance at him. He seems an accessory
after the fact, though the fact
is obscure, as a dad is a closed door.

Dad is alone in the den, courting
exasperation, kissing it on the mouth.

Mom is in the hallway, and now
she's in her son's room, inspecting
his bureau, every drawer a tunnel
she would crawl through, back to the cradle
she lay him in, back to the cold fire
that flickered him into being.

She would palm that flame, drop it
into her purse for safekeeping.

Mom is in love with the idea of her son,
who will love his bureau, supporting it
with his arms bent back, till one day
he asks his wife to lie with it,
to cherish its fullness and bulk, as he does.

A mother is a tunnel. Her son loves her,
the first woman who touched his brow
with tenderness, who is closing now,
with the same care, his bureau drawers,
filled with shirts, folded, as she
has shown him, so the arms bend back.

A Child's Guide to Etiquette

Never put your personal spoon in the common jelly bowl.
Spread your napkin upon your lap. Do not grasp.
Eat what meat your fork can get to; give up the rest of the lobster for lost.
A girl must lay her silver down while still a trifle hungry.
She must not eat unchaperoned.

A boy does not take a girl's arm on the street. The street is no place
      for devotion.
He must not allow his mother to lug the coal or sift the ashes.
If he does, he is a cad. A boy is shiftless, a vulgar bounder. He is not
      excused.
He wears a dark suit, but not in a theatre box. In a box a Tuxedo is worn.
In a box a boy keeps his thoughts to himself.
A girl keeps her hat on until she is seated. The theatre itself wears no hat.

Snow is a hat worn by mountains, the tallest of which do not remove
      the hat in summer.
Sunlight settles like a shawl upon the hills and dewy berry fields.
The sun is not a wag or hail-fellow-well-met. It does not loaf or shirk.
It keeps its face funeral-ready, as you should.
Away you go in the car. Father and Mother. Puff and Baby Sally.
Away you go into the country. Spot and Jane.

Jane is a proper girl. She avoids provincial phrases and slang, as *Yep* and
      boy friend.
She says not *Yes* but *Yes, Mother,* and arranges rosettes in the icing.
She wears a high-collared simple dress and tarries amid the lilac, on her
      head a crown of stars.
She may stop dancing when she wishes. A boy must dance until the
      music ends.
He must scold his bold friend.

A boy is clothed in a purple cloak, is brought up on charges, agrees to
        them with the air of one much pleased. He raises his hat to
        his father.
A girl, in the presence of her father, removes her breasts.
She removes the washbowl's plug so the waste water drains completely.
A boy need not detach his hands, but he must not thrust them into
        his pockets.
A clothes brush must be packed for the train, and a plain dressing
        gown.

Away you go. You are speaking with courtesy and reserve in the
        dining car.
You are slipping off your shoes. You are leaving them for the porter.
The porter will pocket his tip discreetly.
The porter will polish your shoes in the night.

And

They also build small coffins, for dwarves and children.
And I have parallel-parked successfully nineteen times in a row.

Summer's tired; vines untwine; the dusk light couldn't fill an
        abandoned barn.
And I have a handful of quarters left, enough for a box of sparklers.

Hounds bound down from the hills, blood on their muzzles; fields
of asphalt surrounding the fundamentalist church fill with minivans.

And I am fond of rickets, the ring of it. So many kinds of pie!
I have fallen for someone with eyes like baby mice in snow.

I am bedizened with jewels. I am wearing the coat of a dandy.
The bufflehead duck would talk to me, but now he circles,

unsolicitous, masked, upon the pond. I am keen to wait.
I am keen to calculate the number of the mysteries. So far, six.

Brought Back

It was bigger than me
And I felt like a sick child
Dragged by a donkey
Through the myrtle.
            —Vic Chesnutt

I dipped my hand in the wrong pond
plucked the black rose
did not know that I did not know
The red wolf bit me
I bit back
I was pulled by a beast toward bed
blossoms nodding in turn
They took me for one of them
A branch rained water down
It boiled on my brow
I shook beneath a scratchy blanket
The air smelled of bleach and school glue
I was not floating outside my body
Everything floating was in my body
A bird knocked in my chest
Whatever wanted me O mouth
I was held in for a moment
I was not ready but
thank you
silence behind silence
I was almost able to forgive
I had little to forgive
I understood it might not be about forgiveness
Tendrils easing through cracks in my skull
There could be no name for this
Life being emptied of me
No name
A voice asked who I was

Oh thank you before I forget
It broke and
light shot through the blinds
I had answered

Dead End

Then came trucks from the city, groaning around the corner,
six men in coveralls

dispatched at last to honor our dusty
start of a street, pressing asphalt upon it.

I stepped from the woods. The nest of mud and grass
I'd nudged from a branch broke apart in my hands.

Near the neighbors' drained pool,
my sister stood still in a sundress.

One cloud rode high above us. *Forget, forget,*
steam wisped from the blacktop.

My friend whistled once, hiding in the grass
behind his house. I think it was he.

Each ball in each yard rolled under shrubbery,
out of reach. Leaves swiveled on twigs.

At dusk, the workmen's faces blurred
beneath hard hats. Our mothers hollered in turn,

calling us in, all the neighborhood children.
From what world we weren't certain.

Children's Chorus

Our father conceived of us, dealt us like cards to our mother,
then liquefied, seeped into groundwater. Well.
No causal link is inferred. God's in the dirt and desired him.

God's in the crop of squash, in the sinkhole beneath the preschool,
in the swallow's song and the swallowed worm.
He's in the river that would have us drowned.

Born on a wobbly planet, one with a bite out of it, stumbling
suddenly over its surface with little instruction,
our father panicked, improvised. He did his best.

God was in that panic. Praise him. Praise him
who bustles in every molecule, who might have
made us into dolphins, had he thought of it.

And praise our mother, who stayed, whose hurt hands held us
together against her chest, for little cause, given that
God would not have wept had she done otherwise.

Sugar and Sand

It starts as sugar and ends as sand,
starts with a white clot of blossoms,
a bundle in the bassinet, all slobber and possibility.
Then Robert Mitchum's singing hymns in the moonlight,
sauntering along on the horse of a man whose throat he slashed for it.

Sugar, then sand. A girl twirls a phone cord
around her finger, voice of a boy in her ear,
then a widow is backing her Pontiac into the mailbox.

It starts dew-lipped and pink and gets mummified.
It starts as a rose on a bush then wilts in a buttonhole.

The middle's a muddle—
a song in an unplugged jukebox,
a locked valise,
a whiff of Polynesia in Cleveland.
A child waves a paper scepter
while the emperor's statue is loaded onto a flatbed.

A saint's reduced to a tooth and a toebone.
It starts as sugar and ends.
A boy learns the box step, he learns where the cripples are sequestered.

The voice of the Lord is in the trees,
then it's only crickets, it's wind,
it's April clearing its throat of a last bit of winter,
it's sheep beneath the knife.

It's dumbed down, scrubbed to nothing,
last year's sled leaning in the shed on rusty runners,
a dead decade's hats,
a past made of sugar. And sand.
Sand's in the baby formula, in the wedding cake batter.

Sand's in the sugar.
Impossible not to swallow them both, and so
be swallowed, by opening the mouth, by feeling
a first thing touch the tongue.

Rock Polisher

Your father bought it, brought it
to the basement utility closet, waited
while a test pebble tumbled in it.
One week: he'd willed it to brilliance.
The grit kit's yours now, the silicon
carbide pack. Split it, have at it.
Jasper, agate, amethyst crystal,
it'll churn to a luster. Listen
to small rocks grind the big one down.
Stones in the driveway, pry them up, why not,
they'll fit, glass knobs on your mother's
bathroom cabinet, your baseball
and mitt, polish them, polish that
zero-win Peewee League season.
The thing your sister said and then
took back, you still have it, polish it,
polish the snowless Christmas
when all you'd hoped for was snow.
It's way past lights-out now, you're crouched
above the barrel, feeding it
your school shoes, your haircut
in eighth grade—flat bangs
to the bridge of your nose—the moment
that girl on the track team touched
your wrist, then kept her fingers there,
the way you loved dumbly
and do. If the sun's up, it's nothing,
you're polishing, you're pouring in
the ocean rolling rocks into cobbles
too slowly, and the sky, it was
Mozart's, was Christ's sky,
no matter, dismantle it, drop it
into the tumbler, and you too, get in there
with your dad and your mom and the cat,
one by one, the whole family,
and God's mercy, perfect at last.

Cruising Lake City

Car full of fuckups, unlaureled easy ironists,
'twas witlack we suffered, 'twas sixteen
and Emerson, Lake, and Palmer
and inexact timing, fingers drumming the dash
and seat backs, a kind of piety in that,
Scott's mom's dilapidated Plymouth,
burger bags, bullhorn for public wisecracks
in Kurt's Pakistani accent, 'twas certitude
and love, love
like a fox that gnawed at our chests, Al
rolling his window down on Beth's block
to place in each mailbox
a tiny mustard pack, I
slouched in the back, a mistake with a face—
what fuse in Sue Cardinal's heart
had blown so it could not want me, so it would not
grieve if I kneeled and died
beneath her window, unhouseled, how about that,
night fog like wool in the trees,
none of us mentioned it, rudderless
we rode, without
although, without because, just
this, this, this
and us, which was almost enough.

Hubbub and Ruck

I'm one prince. It takes a hundred princes
just to reroute traffic these days. An easy

chaos has come, a quickening. More laws
against loitering, more loitering, more blips

on the radar screen, building permits, hints
of crimson in the sunset, caterpillars

writhing in dirt beneath the trees.
A recalibration. A roused appetite.

The deer have made a sport of it,
leaving their bodies by the highwayside,

crumpled, like dropped coats. More racks
of Turkish fashions, winks and backslaps,

fire scorching the cathedral stones. It's too
too, a sleight-of-hand, past justice.

Death can't dazzle with its steamy vat
of tar. All the cabooses abandoned

on the tracks—Lord, receive our thanks.
Flags collapsing, bellying in the breeze.

The thousand cows bleeding in the fields.
They're getting up. They're OK, really.

In a Body

You can lead a boy to the altar rail. You can make him kneel.
Instructed in shame, I bloomed with red petals of it.
I understood my heart was filled with dirt.

In a body, you're obvious: straggle-haired, near-naked, mucking
out the stalls
or whacking a bent wheel with a hammer
or stumbling up the aisle into the projector light, head expanding,
devouring the screen.

In the end, the dead will get their bodies back, their cups will be
filled with wine.
One can believe anything!
My toy train rattled through a canyon molded from flour and water.

At fourteen I wore tank tops adorned with beer logos.
At sixteen I felt like a mobile robot in rough terrain.
I dreamed of hawking my grin on television.

Even the prettiest body's owner abandons it. Then who wants it
around?
It's what's gone that we were looking at.
My body's grown taller than most, gut-plump, a little itchy.

When I got here I was sticky and small, I sang a loud flat note.
I'll hit that note till Jesus cringes.
I'll leave the rest on my plate but eat the meat.

Once

Once, a black panic of birds scattering from a tree.
Some finger flicked them.

Once, a fox at the far edge of a field:
my father, back from battle, back with plain talk.

In lamplight, in the pages
of my math book, a gold moth.

But it was he they eased down into the dirt—
I saw it—he never recovered. Once,

rain. After, a cold sun, earthworms
in the runoff. Pharaoh hardened his heart.

Angels at Seattle

No bootprint in the moondust yet, 1969, July, I choose that time,
the shadowy concrete stairwell, the cool of it,
my one small step

into the sun-shocked stadium, thwack of ball in mitt, field bright
with Pilots and Angels. I choose
the idea of it,

my guide the ancient usher—yellow vest, freckled hands—
so distracted, examining my father's ticket stub,
he does not feel

the pearl of sweat sliding down his forehead toward
the ridge of his nose. The Pilots had a bad year,
weighed anchor, sailed

for Wisconsin. No cause then for Angels to play here. No matter.
It's summer. I'm in my hometown, keeping
my eye on the ball

of sweat at the tip of the usher's nose, stalled there,
wobbling. I'm choosing to watch it
refuse to fall.

Shrink Wrap

Can't get these western seventies teenage clothes off.
I started as a twitchy witless newborn rat pup
thrilled with the nipple and milk—willingly, forthwith,

I slipped the Tangerine Dream concert T-shirt
over my skinniness, tried the wide white belt.
Tried Tang. Tried my new heart, inscrutable

as calculus and obstinately blue, not
as you'd notice. I was pink-skinned from pudding
and meatloaf, I counted down to liftoff,

counted down the hits, was too young
to be a jungle grunt on his stomach in the mud.
I'd like to pay for that now, pay for the summers—

glad endless meadows of television—pay
for my paltry safe American belated boy life.
Bobby Kennedy didn't hurt me. Nixon didn't.

Lynn did, when she leaned her head against Peter's
at the pencil sharpener. Lennon did, when his skin
let the bullets in. I knew then I could weep

for a stranger. Or my records. Otherwise—and what
is the penance for this?—I lay on a raft and drifted
across the lake of myself, little lidless blind eye.

At this late date, what is mine to offer in payment
for such debt? Steely Dan's second album, perhaps?
Never played. Mint. Original shrink wrap.

My Ancestors on Either Side

Grimed and bearded sealskin stitchers,
sledge drivers, jug-drunk
benighted pissers into fire,
nomadic herders of reindeer, hunks of whom
they slathered with lard after boiling.
They roasted the shrike on a stick.
Lots of buckets.
Lots of trudging through dung to club the pig
then get ground out and cling, pink-knuckled,
to the floating Holy Virgin's robe—
she strained at their weight, then
kicked them off and lifted into the blue.

How weary they must have been of not living
in the twenty-first century, not even the flintlock yet,
no Sinatra wafting through the coffee shop
in waves, miraculously (as he has to
now, being as gone as they are),
though surely they donned a gay getup
on gonfalon-raising day
and crooned some tune they'd come to love
as I too used to set a jaunty cap
upon my head and chant "I Can't Believe
That You're in Love with Me," motoring over this soil
so many toiled upon, then stayed put in.

O distant sisters, uncles, the stars
are strewn like dice—you'd recognize them.
Summer's come again and gone, like sea spray.
You and I would have some tales to trade
about such things that happen in a trice, a phrase
in fashion before my time, after yours.

Appearing in a trice, a stranger
shaded the lady's face with a parasol.
In a trice, the undertow took my wife.
I became the sort of man
who wheels a TV toward the table
and sits in its noisy glow
as he gnaws meat from a bone.

Late Appraisal

I won't go soon into the Hall of Valor.
The first thing I did with that bird in me was feed it a stone.

When they come, they can have the jangle in my pocket.
I'll lie on my back in the box and be quiet.

It's something, being an onion in the dirt:
white fist, white eye that won't see.

It's something, to have been inadequate
and made it look like stubbornness.

Dream: Sympathy

Blighted field. Broken cornstalks. Mice skitter
in furrows, squeal at my feet. Their eyes
bleed at the rims. Hunger? They don't

belong here. They've entered my myth
of origins, my month of eating hard red berries.
I've hidden a last one under my tongue.

Then: a sacristy. I'm gold-robed, ready
for Holy Orders, ready for song. My mouth
opens; motion pesters the air, birds

flap at me, hundreds, from nowhere—
they screech, crimson throat-feathers
flashing. They are unappeasable.

My Almost-Daughter, My Nearly-Was-Son

Those overtime nights in the ice factory, eyeing gauges, greasing gears:
that's one thing. And the hours of clarinet lessons.

All that rain that blathered on the patio, leaves
lifting and twisting, a demented semaphore. I hired myself

to crack that code, kept busy not conceiving you. I peopled
the past, got safely sad about it. I hammered together

a hut in the back of my brain to crawl inside and rest
from the labor of making it. My almost-daughter, my nearly-was-son,

I was frugal, I made you wait till you grew
into the idea of waiting. See? These words hurt no one.

My Ghosts

And is this my sister in her yellow shift, taciturn, scratching at the
        dirt of the frozen garden as if in search of her father?

And is he here, in the dark garage, bending as he did over the
        Christmas ham, unable to carve it now, the hands that hurt
        him in this world turned to vapor?

And have they come to instruct me, and wordlessly?

And are these my brides, arm in arm in air, a silent choir?

Are they here to comfort, or be comforted?

Afloat amid limbs of the pine, are these my ancient aunts and
        uncles, lurching, stomping inaudibly in some Nordic
        peasant dance, and were they ever this ungrim?

And has my grandmother joined them? Is her husband fingering
        a keyless clarinet, winking at me as he was wont to do?

And is that my cue to speak? Or to listen differently?

Skink

Flits beneath a rotten log,
hint and slither, thought

I can't follow. Skittery finger
pointing elsewhere, while summer

fits its silver suit onto the year's
black bones again.

Permanence, impermanence—
one loves them both, one says.

The conspiracy. Yes. Noon light
clean as an equal sign.

But to believe so and haul
such heaviness, clattering

when I'm handled, like a sack of knives...
Blank is his eye, no help there.

The tail an implausible blue.
It breaks off in your hand.

Flowers of the World, with Full-Color Plates

Reddish-purple petals, tongues drunk on wine, that's the wake-robin
trillium.

The Chinese hat plant looks like stooped workers in a rice field.

Long pretty ropes, enough to hang a town, that's love-lies-bleeding.

Downcast-girl-in-the-buttercups, we call it, though it's a kind of
begonia, what's said and what's seen rooting always in
separate soil.

Sun snagged on barbed wire, what I was when she left me,
mind-in-a-mist.

Roused by dusk, the bush ablaze within minutes, that's the evening
primrose.

I doubted God's-pity, though I wore it in my buttonhole.

Bloodroot's eyes close in the dark.

Buds that blossom in sequence, the first flower dying so the last
might live, the freesia.

Petals pointing upward, skywriting-at-night.

June reddens with curtsies-to-the-queen.

Midsummer, suddenly duncecaps dot the hills, trap-door-in-Christ's-
tomb all over, my doubtful mouth opens.

Love, or Something

The way, at last, a sloop goes sailorless and bobs at the dock, swathed
        in darkness,
the way waves swell and, swelling, slay themselves—
water, whatever you want, I want to want that.

A nickel's in the till, then it's not, it's in a pocket, forgotten,
and the pocket's in a laundry chute. A puddle's in the parking lot, drying
to a ring of rust, asphalt buckling from something under it.

Conspiracy of earth and air in me, slip me your secret, I won't fret,
you want me stoneground, I want to want that. I want
the fire to find me ready. Let it be not scorn or pluck

I summon as I'm swallowed—I'm sick of pluck. Let it be love,
or something like it, assuming love is to the purpose, assuming
I'm not being maudlin, merely human, to bring love up.

Last Words

The night sky's a black stretch limo, boss in the back
behind tinted glass. You could say that.

Down here's a dungeon, up there's the glittering
ring of keys in the sentry's fist. The self

exists. Beauty too. But they're elsewhere.
You could say that. Or not speak till commanded to.

Dawn, alone on the porch, I watch
the one map unfold and flatten before me—

same toppled TV antenna in the berry vines,
same cardinal, bright wound in the pasture grass.

My wound is my business. I've wearied of it.
From now on, morning will be attended

by its own noises only, evening will approach
without palms in its path. Let the horses

steam in the field, the sun-struck
river blanch. I'm boarding the troop train.

Postulates

On a mountain, we don't see the mountain.

Whatever is half as heavy is twice as light.

We live in air, it lives in us.

A bee trapped in a cabinet responds with willed indifference, then panic.

My father giving up: shattered cup, cat nudging the dry water bowl.

We are threads in the seams of eternity's shirt.

Bone, coat, contact lenses.

I woke on my thirteenth birthday, mouth slack, my hand a black leaf.

No, I woke. The rest I've forgotten.

The heart is not a match head: it catches fire again and again.

Time revises. We revise.

We are in the seams.

Conference call. Cigarette. Cuff link, skin, water, father, air.

Too Much in the Sun

My father was a man of science, tinker
by trade, snake handler. He landed

his Spitfire in the fog without
the aid of instruments, was flogged

on the quarterdeck. Slept in boxcars,
being an Okie. Not really. Verily,

early did he rise and join
the assembly of clouds, and did not submit

his diary for examination. Took that
with him. He tired of the sun

burying itself at sea each day
then resurrecting, tired of the way

it peels the shadow off a water tower
as if it were a surgeon's glove. Neat trick.

Pretending to account for him, I account
for myself in secret. I see that. I saw

my face in the shine of my shoes
and met no one else in my travels—no dwarf

squirmed from a cranny in the ground
to demand that I answer a riddle.

I demanded it myself. A blank
sun's my clue, a grackle in the sumac

making a racket, little sense in it.
Little sense in presuming to speak for it.

My father knew that—he who keeps mute
in the world beyond, unless that's this one.

November Song

Now, night coming down in flakes of ash, leaves
clumped, wasting in the culvert, where

is the grasshopper who accordioned all summer,
fiddled and swigged, made merry, carried on?

He carries on. No joy shall incur a debt
under my administration. The last end,

the sea receiving us, heaving us
up as tangled black weedy stuff—not

in the budget. And the unctuous
undone by love, they'll earn a medal for it.

Holy Mess

At the tone the time will be
not now. No matter. Namu,
the killer whale, dead
from too much taming, dead, some luck,
on Jenny's birthday in 1966
(there went the aquarium party), Namu
swims within me, nothing leaves
completely. I rode in my dad's
white Dodge once, now the Dodge rides
inside me; that inky, inebriant scent
of expectation in my head is *The Amazing*
Flight to the Mushroom Planet
before I'd read it; the dusk of 1970
comes down within me still, comes down
upon our neighborhood hiding games,
the whole world in hiding—till 1977
and Elvis Costello's *My Aim Is True,*
its dorky guilty intelligent venom and liberty,
record descended from heaven to wash
clean the earth of all other records, it spins
within me, amid the clutter and whatnot
without which I am monkey—
the hodgepodge of oddments
whose deep design I might have glimpsed
in physics class had I not been baffled
and distracted in it. But Mrs. Myers' class
is in me, too: the simple shoes, the dignified
fierce eyes—O Mrs. Myers, I turn myself
in, I am Rodion Raskolnikov: here
is the ax, hair on the bloody blade,
here are the beers I'm downing
with my brother, 1980, midnight
by the railroad tracks, our topics being
Dylan and Berryman and the big

unknowable nothing, about which I elect
to be safely wry, unable to be smart
or to just shut up, like the infinite dark
wheatfields that surround us,
and one of us says
this, this moment, us: it might be
summoned back into being in a poem
years from now, made moist
with retrospective significance—yes,
as hard Christmas candy in a dish
is significant, for it is in me, as Al and Paul
are in me, and Holly, Holly, her garlic
from the garden, her lotion and slick sheets
like an oil spill across 1983,
like mop water I slopped onto the floor
of the nursing home kitchen and let lap
against the ten-pound tubs of applesauce,
which also live within me
as does my first wife, as does my second,
as do seven houses and the small
rented place I'm in now, sifting
through my holy mess to find
the poem in it, a grave, preposterous sun
blazing upon it all, upon all
holy messes equally, the same sun
that has not budged at least
since 1963, as I can testify personally.

What He Left Behind

Jam jar of cigarette ends and ashes on his workbench,
hammer he nailed our address to a stump with,
balsawood steamship, half-finished—

is that him, waving from the stern? Well, good luck to him.
Slur of sunlight filling the backyard, August's high wattage,
white blossoming, it's a curve, it comes back. My mother

in a patio chair, leaning forward, squinting, threading
her needle again, her eye lifts to the roof, to my brother,
who stands and jerks his arm upward—he might be

insulting the sky, but he's only letting go
a bit of green, a molded plastic soldier
tied to a parachute, thin as a bread bag, it rises, it arcs

against the blue—good luck to it—my sister and I below,
heads tilted back as we stand in the grass, good
luck to all of us, still here, still in love with it.

Acknowledgments

Grateful acknowledgment is made to the editors of the journals in which these poems first appeared, sometimes in earlier versions:

AGNI Online: "Last Words"
Antioch Review: "Prayer Before Sleep," "Shrink Wrap"
Barrow Street: "Late Appraisal," "Postulates," "Self-Portrait"
Bellingham Review: "The Case Against Me," "Children's Chorus," "Dead
    End," "This Time"
Colorado Review: "Once"
Crazyhorse: "Sugar and Sand," "The Woods"
Georgia Review: "In a Body," "My Ancestors on Either Side," "Too Much
    in the Sun"
Image: "Brought Back"
New England Review: "Hubbub and Ruck," "Rock Polisher"
New Orleans Review: "And," "School Carnival," "Skink"
Paris Review: "A Child's Guide to Etiquette," "My Father's Curriculum
    Vitae," "Testament," "Toward a Full Accounting," "Where I
    Come From"
Pleiades: "Holy Mess," "What He Left Behind" (under the title "What My
    Father Left Behind")
Ploughshares: "Dream: Natural Law," "Love, or Something"
Prairie Schooner: "Black"
Red Mountain Review: "Family Vacation," "Postmortem"
Rhino: "Cruising Lake City," "The Fall"
Slate: "My Almost-Daughter, My Nearly-Was-Son," "Vanishing Act"
Southern Humanities Review: "Climbing Down," "Fourth Grade Science,"
    "Having Crept from My Bed," "Hopeful Green Stuff"
Verb: "Flowers of the World, with Full-Color Plates," "Thirty-Year Elegy"

"Rock Polisher" was reprinted in *The Best American Poetry 2008* (Scribner)
"Love, or Something" was reprinted in *The Pushcart Prize XXXIII: Best of
    the Small Presses 2009* and the *Alhambra Poetry Calendar 2008,*
    edited by Shafiq Naz
"Sugar and Sand" and "Hopeful Green Stuff" were reprinted in the
    Alhambra Poetry Calendar 2006 and *2007,* respectively
"Bureau Inspection" first appeared in the exhibition catalog *Tom Aprile,*
    UM Gallery, Seoul, South Korea, 2007

This book was written with the generous support and encouragement of the National Endowment for the Arts, the Corporation of Yaddo, Butler University, Auburn University, and the University of Virginia. For invaluable advice on revision, thanks to Lawrence Raab and, at *Barrow Street*, Peter Covino, Talvikki Ansel, and Richard Hoffman. Thanks also to Phillis Levin for choosing the manuscript.

Gratitude and love to Russ Scott, second father.

And Alessandra Lynch. Always Alessandra. And Milo.

Notes

"Vanishing Act": The italicized line is from "No Matter What" by Badfinger.

"Hopeful Green Stuff": The poem's title is from Walt Whitman. The italicized line is from "O-o-h Child" by The Five Stairsteps.

"Bureau Inspection" is for Tom Aprile.

"A Child's Guide to Etiquette" owes a debt to *Etiquette Every Child Should Know,* by Mary E. Clark and Margery Closey Quigley (Doubleday, Doran, & Co., 1939), and to *We Come and Go,* by William S. Gray, Dorothy Baruch, and Elizabeth Rider Montgomery (Scott, Foresman, & Co., 1968).

"Brought Back": The epigraph is from Vic Chesnutt's song "Myrtle."

"Sugar and Sand" is for Dorine Jennette, who recommended writing a poem with this title. Mitchum's scene is in *The Night of the Hunter.*

"Too Much in the Sun" is for Bob Clark, who gave me the assignment of writing a poem with this title (which is from *Hamlet,* Act I, Scene 2).

Barrow Street Poetry

Black Leapt In
Chris Forhan (2009)

Boy with Flowers
Ely Shipley (2008)

Gold Star Road
Richard Hoffman (2007)

Hidden Sequel
Stan Sanvel Rubin (2006)

Annus Mirabilis
Sally Ball (2005)

A Hat on the Bed
Christine Scanlon (2004)

Hiatus
Evelyn Reilly (2004)

3.14159+
Lois Hirshkowitz (2004)

Selah
Joshua Corey (2003)